DR. LEE JAMPOLSKY

smile
for no good reason

Simple Things You Can Do To Get Happy **NOW**

Table of Contents

Introduction. 4

Principle Number One:
The essence of our being is love.. 9

Principle Number Two:
Health is inner peace. Healing is letting go of fear.. 17

Principle Number Three:
Giving and receiving are the same.. 31

Principle Number Four:
We can let go of the past and of the future.. 43

Principle Number Five:
Now is the only time there is, and each instant is for giving. 53

Principle Number Six:
We can learn to love ourselves and others by forgiving rather than judging.. . . . 61

Principle Number Seven:
We can become love finders rather than fault finders. 71

Principle Number Eight:
We can choose and direct ourselves
to be peaceful inside regardless of what is happening outside. 85

Principle Number Nine:
We are students and teachers to each other. 97

Principle Number Ten:
We can focus on the whole of life rather than the fragments. 109

Principle Number Eleven:
Since love is eternal, death need not be viewed as fearful. 121

Principle Number Twelve:
We can always perceive ourselves and
others as either extending love or giving a call for help.. 129

Conclusion 138

About the Author 140

Introduction

Attitudinal Healing has touched the hearts of dying children and adults, eased the pain of citizens ravaged by war, redirected Fortune 500 companies, captured the attention of world leaders, assisted medical experts in major universities, been welcomed by Nobel Peace laureates, and yet most people have still not heard of Attitudinal Healing. This, in part, is because there is nothing commercial about it. It is a quiet wisdom for those who want it. In the high-tech information age such basic knowledge can easily go unnoticed.

This book presents clear and concise ways—that you can begin right now—to begin living a happier and more meaningful life. You will learn to feel more peaceful and be more productive by replacing the automatic ways you react from fear with new perceptions of yourself and the world.

A primary teaching of Attitudinal Healing is: Nothing needs to change in your life situation or the world in order for you to have peace of mind. At first, such a notion may seem implausible. This idea is foreign to the typical way of thinking, which states, "If you're unhappy, change something in your life. Change jobs, buy something new, find a different relationship."

It is easy to become sidetracked and stressed by a multitude of little tasks and problems, and to lose sight of what really matters. In this increasingly complicated world, what is needed is to remind yourself of what is most precious. This book offers simple and practical ways to be happy by approaching life with a different attitude.

Have you noticed that the changes you make in your life are often only short-term fixes? Regardless of how you modify your life, do stress and conflict soon creep back in? Changing life circumstances without addressing your thinking is like painting over rust: It will look great for a while, but eventually the old rust will slowly break through the new paint. By addressing your attitudes, nothing more and nothing less, whatever changes you make will contribute to your lasting happiness rather than lead to another disappointment or failure.

Attitudinal Healing is a way of having happiness without having to change your social status, religion, spouse, or the amount in your bank account. Attitudinal Healing is a way to go through your day responding to life's challenges with peace of mind rather than with fear, anger and guilt. It has helped thousands of people and can now help you.

My father, Dr. Gerald Jampolsky, as a means of helping children and their families suffering from catastrophic illness, originally developed Attitudinal Healing in the seventies. The principles of Attitudinal Healing were originally inspired by *A Course In Miracles*, a three-volume set of books published by the Foundation for Inner Peace. I began working with these ideas in 1977 while in graduate school, and they continue to guide and improve my life. I have also seen the principles help transform the lives of people from diverse backgrounds, cultures, and religions.

This book is divided into one section for each of the twelve principles of Attitudinal Healing. Each section contains vignettes to help apply the principles to daily living. It is my hope the short writings will resonate with something deep within you, and that you will find yourself smiling for no good reason.

"Love releases us into the realm of divine imagination, where the soul is expanded … Love allows a person to see the true angelic nature of another person, the halo, the aureole of divinity."

THOMAS MOORE

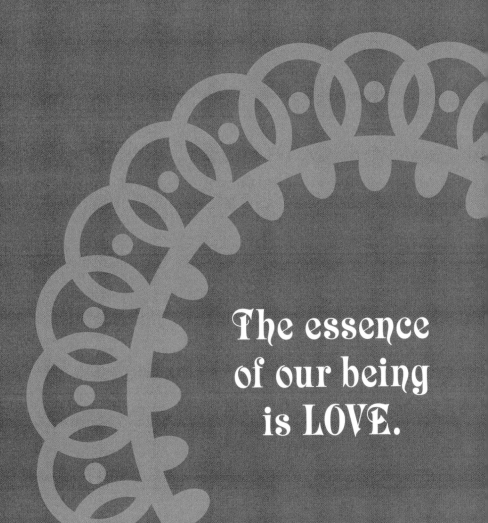

The essence
of our being
is LOVE.

SPEND MORE OF YOUR LIFE TRYING TO UNDERSTAND OTHER PEOPLE'S VIEWS THAN TRYING TO SELL THEM ON YOUR OWN

What did you want most as a child? To be loved? And what could most effectively communicate that you were loved? Was it not to be listened to with interest and caring? Though the world might seem much more complicated as an adult, nothing has changed in terms of your most basic needs. There is no greater gift you can give a person than listening to him or her.

Despite popular opinion, the goal of listening is not to figure out how the other person is wrong and how you can make him or her see it your way. Nor is it to figure out what the problem is and fix it. The goal of authentic listening is to love.

People are so busy in our culture that lack of listening is epidemic. One of the most common complaints in couples' therapy is, "I just want to be heard. He/she doesn't understand me." Teenagers often state, "I am tired of only hearing what I do wrong. You have no idea what my life is really like." Younger children act out because they experience their parent's lack of listening. Employees often know their company well and have good ideas, yet rather than being listened to, they are often handed a new policy to follow. Officials elected to represent the people often forget to listen and instead they promote agendas of their own.

Listening can be mistaken for doing nothing. This is because you can believe that taking some sort of physical action is always necessary. Listening authentically is active, and is one of the most powerful actions you can initiate in your life.

Try a little experiment. Instead of taking some physical action, focus on actively listening more. Active listening means that you listen to other people with the full intention of understanding them. For this experiment, let go of any criticism you might have of the other person. Don't try to figure out any solutions to what he or she is saying. Simply listen. Your eye contact, relaxed body posture, and unhurried mood all communicate, "I want to know your perspective and your experience." If you give verbal responses, let them be centered on trying to understand the other person, as opposed to arguing or offering your opinion or advice.

This experiment can be challenging because really listening requires slowing down and being present. It is worth the effort because there is no greater gift, especially to those people whom you most love.

Practice active listening
and other people will feel loved and accepted by you.
And, you will feel like you were just given wings.

YOU ARE MORE IMPORTANT THAN YOUR "TO DO" LIST

———— ‹●› ————

Chances are excellent that the day you die your "to do" list will not be empty. You could either kill yourself trying to get it all done, or never start living because there is always something else to do first. There is another way.

Not only are you more important than your list of things to do, so are other people in your life. It is easy to put off relating to your self, spouse, kids, friends and animals—decide not to. Decide to relate.

At least three times every day take a moment and ask yourself what is really important. Have the wisdom and the courage to build your life around your answer.

I recently came across the following quote that puts priorities in perspective. I don't know where it originated, but its simple wisdom gets my attention.

If you knew today was your last day to live
who would you call, and what would you say?
What are you waiting for?

CREATE A PERSONAL MISSION STATEMENT

Have you noticed that one day something can set you off and another day you take the same thing in stride? This is because the way you react is completely dependent upon what thoughts you hold in your mind.

A sailboat without a keel and rudder will be blown wherever the winds and tides direct. In the same way, without a stated purpose the winds of life can easily blow you where they will. You may end up feeling that you have few choices, or worse, feeling like a victim.

One of the first things an effective new business will do, or an established one that desires new direction and success, is create a mission statement. An effective mission statement is short and direct. It is the rudder of the vessel, keeping it on track in both challenging and successful times.

Similarly, creating a personal mission statement can give your life new meaning and keep you from falling into familiar patterns or habits. To begin, set aside some time and write down whatever comes to your mind when you ask yourself, "What is important to me? How do I want to live my life?" Next, write a few summary sentences that embody all you have said on your list. Sharpen it up and you have a mission statement.

About five years ago, by asking myself the above questions, I developed my personal mission statement: Be as kind as you can possibly be. Inspire compassion in others. These two sentences have often helped me resist the temptation to become angry, brought me back on track when I have become defensive, helped me have patience with my children, and led me to be of service to others. There is nothing dazzling about my mission statement, any more than there is about a keel hidden beneath a boat that provides stability in turbulent seas. Nonetheless, my mission statement has helped me enormously in keeping my life directed.

Having a mission statement for your life is a quick and essential way to bring your existence into focus and give you purpose. Develop one today. Write it down on several index cards and put them places where you will see them often. For a while, attempt to remind yourself every hour of what your mission statement is.

Some people don't know where they want to go but complain a lot about not getting there. Decide not to be one of them.

"Fears hate more than anything else to be defeated.
They will try to invade your new truth like a virus,
telling you what you can't do, not what you can do,
telling you what you can't be, not what you are ...
Don't listen."

SUZE ORMAN

Health is inner peace.
Healing is letting go of fear.

CREATE A BOUNCER FOR YOUR MIND

———— ◄●► ————

Attitudinal Healing defines health as inner peace, and recognizes that healing is letting go of fear-based thoughts. This definition acknowledges that health and healing are of the mind, and are not based on the condition of your body, your bank account, or your job. Mother Teresa—who worked with starvation, death, and dying—once commented that there was more spiritual deprivation on the streets of New York than on the streets of Calcutta. This statement acknowledges that one can have a youthful, attractive, strong body, a nice suit, and a cell phone and be far from healthy. In short, health and healing are a result of what thoughts you hold in your mind.

There is a very logical progression in this definition:

If you want to be healthy, devote yourself to peace of mind.

The way you do this is by becoming aware of what thoughts are fear-based and then letting them go.

When I was in college, a popular bar offered me a job as a bouncer. My job description was straightforward: Determine at the door who was "appropriate" for entrance into the bar and who was not. (At the time my friends said having me as a bouncer was like having the rooster guard the henhouse.) When I made a mistake and let in a "troublemaker," it was then my task to tactfully, and without incident remove the troublemaker from the establishment.

Similarly, it is important to be able to determine what thoughts to let into your mind, and which to keep out. Think of your mind as an "establishment" that is committed to peace of mind. Develop a watchful part of your mind to be a "bouncer" at the door who has the sole purpose of determining whether a certain perception, thought, or belief is conducive to your peace of mind. If it is, gladly let it in. If not, send it on its way. Of course, there is the chance that your bouncer will make a mistake. In this case, it is necessary to tactfully, and without incident, remove the "trouble-making thought" from your mind.

Unfortunately, your ego (i.e., the fearful part of yourself that believes you are separate from God) has its own type of bouncer. This bouncer tells you it will keep you safe, but it does so by holding onto thoughts of resentment, hatred, guilt, and fear. It tries to sell you on its insane view of safety by telling you things like:

"Getting even will make you feel better."

"Beat yourself up for your mistakes and you won't repeat them."

"Stay angry with, or even hate, those who have done you wrong and you will find security."

What the ego is really concerned with is keeping your true nature, love, hidden from your awareness.

Create a positive bouncer for your mind. You will become healthy as you take charge of your own thoughts. If ever you find yourself with resentful, guilty, or excessively angry thoughts do the following:

Ask yourself: "Will these thoughts lead me to have peace of mind?"

Clearly say, "I am devoted to health, and these thoughts are unhealthy."

*When you see
the relationship between
your thoughts and your experience in life,
you have taken the largest step toward health.*

ATTITUDE IS ALL THAT MATTERS

Have you ever noticed that two people can confront the same circumstances with very different reactions? This is a matter of attitude and nothing else. Freedom is being able to say, "Rich or poor, alone or with a mate, physically healthy or not, employed or laid off, I believe that peace of mind is possible."

We have all experienced what it is like to be having a perfectly fine day and have a situation or crisis arise that sends us into a tailspin. It may be something small like a traffic jam making us late, or something more severe like the loss of a job. Our response can seem automatic.

Though at first it may be difficult to accept, freedom depends on recognizing that you're not upset because of what occurred, you are upset because of how you perceive the situation. Key to Attitudinal Healing is recognizing that you are not a victim of the world.

Another way of saying this is: There is absolutely nothing in the world that has the power to ruin your day. If you are upset, it is because you have directed your mind to be so. Initially these truths can be hard to accept because you have become so accustomed to giving your power away. Every time you blame another person for your unhappiness, you are giving your power away. Stop blaming and start healing.

How you perceive a situation will determine your experience and your reaction. Let's imagine that you have a favorite coffeehouse that you frequent. The staff knows your name and always has a warm and friendly greeting as you walk through the door. An extremely grumpy woman whom you have never seen before serves you this particular morning. She appears preoccupied rather than caring about you or what she is doing. As she pours your hot coffee, a good portion spills in your lap. Despite your jumping in shock, no apology follows. Your experience is anger: both toward the waitress and the owner, Joe, for hiring such an incompetent person. Then, a friend of yours at the next booth says, "Isn't it great that Joe hired her!"

"Great! Are you out of your mind? She just spilled hot coffee in my lap and walked away," you reply with your best indignant voice.

"Oh, you didn't hear the story?" your friend whispers.

"What story?" you angrily reply, still drying off your new slacks, wondering how you will go through the day looking as though you wet your pants.

"Yeah, Joe didn't know her from Adam. He read in the paper that her husband had died last month in a car accident. Apparently her husband's health insurance stopped, and she was looking for another job in order to pay for her sixteen-year old son's chemotherapy for leukemia," your friend responds.

Now, you still have hot coffee in your lap, but are you still angry? Unlikely.

The only thing that shifted was your perception and attitude. Through discovering a reason to be compassionate, your entire experience changed—and there are always reasons to be compassionate.

An important part of healing (i.e., letting go of fear) is developing compassion. Instead of going out in the world and finding plenty of reasons to be upset, go out and discover reasons to extend love. There are thousands of reasons waiting for you right now. A helpful thought to remember is that a miracle is nothing more than allowing an old grievance to become a current compassion.

If you ever run short on reasons to be compassionate, remember there is always one good reason: It makes you feel better than anything else you could do.

When you are upset, remind yourself the cause of your discomfort is your own attitude. This is freedom.

THE WISDOM OF
THE CHINESE FINGER PUZZLE

In some novelty stores you will find Chinese finger puzzles, small and colorful woven sheaths whose ends you insert both index fingers into. To free yourself, your first reaction is most likely to pull them out. As you may have experienced, this will only tighten the sheath around your fingers.

This is exactly what painful states of mind are like. If you try to get away from past pain, current problems, or an anticipated difficult future by running away or avoiding, the suffering has a way of getting a tighter grip on your life.

The way out of the Chinese finger puzzle offers us four steps that are applicable to our daily life:

1. Be careful not to overreact.
2. Relax and breathe deeply.
3. Move with thoughtful intention and awareness.
4. Once free, only do it again if you really need the practice.

Being careful not to overreact means that you become less controlled by your automatic responses. In order not to have an automatic response, it is important to react to what is happening now, not what was happening then (five minutes, five days, or five years ago), or what might be happening later.

To have inner peace, become an "Is-Now Person" in your reactions, not a "Was-Then Person" or a "Might-Be Person." "Is-Nows" have a lot more fun and joy than "Was-Thens" or "Might-Bes." "Is-Nows" are also much more efficient and productive because they are dealing with what is, not what was or might be. If you are dealing with what is, you will find it easier to respond with kindness, which creates solutions. If you are coming from what was or what might be, you will probably be operating from fear, and you can end up creating problem after problem.

The most important tool in becoming an "Is-Now" is to direct your mind to relax, and your breath to deepen. Learn, where applicable, to have at least a 30-second pause between what is happening and your reaction to it. Ask yourself, "Do I want to respond with tension, anxiety, and fear from what was, or with love, compassion, and understanding to what is?"

You have probably noticed that sometimes you can solve a particular problem or situation, only to find yourself in the same or similar circumstances again. You may feel that this is a result of what is happening in the world, not what is happening in your mind. Look again. Once you take your fingers out of the puzzle, don't put them back in unless you want to. Many people will say, "Well, the problem just presented itself again and I had to take care of it." Don't go along with that thinking any longer. Many of your problems in life are because you agree to participate in them.

Problems are like dance partners: When they tap you on the shoulder to cut in on your peace of mind, be discerning. Learn to say no to some of your problems and you will have a more peaceful life.

DO NOT
automatically react.

If you feel your life tightening

around you, pause.

Direct your mind and actions

in the direction you choose.

"When I was in London,
I went to see the homeless people
where our sisters have a soup kitchen.
One man, who was living in a cardboard box,
held my hand and said,
'It's been a long time since I
felt the warmth of a human hand.'"

MOTHER TERESA

Giving and
receiving
are the same.

YOUR DEFENSES BRING WHAT THEY WERE MEANT TO GUARD AGAINST

There is a wonderful little piece of magic that you can discover anytime, anywhere: When you give unconditional love, you will receive it— magnified and with no delay. The great thing about this principle is that it is so easily tested, and nothing is required of you that you don't already possess.

Attitudinal Healing teaches that it is through giving and receiving that you will discover health and happiness. It also recognizes a basic spiritual truth: Giving and receiving are the same. The largest obstacle to giving and receiving is the fearful voice inside of you that makes statements such as, "If I give, I will just be taken advantage of again." Or, "If I give, you'd better be grateful and do something nice for me in return." These are your defenses. You created them because you want love and don't want to be hurt. The problem is your defenses keep love from you and bring pain to your life.

Defenses are ways of thinking and acting which you believe will protect you from being hurt. Yet in actuality, your defenses will ultimately bring what they were meant to guard against.

Have you ever known somebody who dreams of having a great relationship, but believes that nobody can be trusted and therefore treats everyone with a good deal of distrust? Not surprisingly, they don't find someone to love and trust fully— few want to stick around while being treated like they can't be trusted. Or, have you known people who have had a very painful past, and as a result, put tremendous defensive energy into not letting something similar happen again? They usually end up alone or with someone who repeats the pattern of their pain. For example, most adults who grew up in an alcoholic family swear that the same havoc will not be in their lives again. And yet, without awareness, their defenses will often bring them what they were meant to guard against: They either marry a chemically dependent person or become one.

Your defenses can be hard to get rid of because you may have strong, even seemingly logical, arguments for why you need them. Try a little experiment. Instead of being afraid of not getting what you want, give what it is that you do want. This creates a force in your life that will make your dreams come true and your defenses melt away. Remember, in giving do not focus on the other person's reaction. Rather, place your awareness on the universal law that you receive what you give.

Your defenses are dams that block miracles from flowing naturally in your life.

FOR ONE WEEK, GO OUT OF YOUR WAY TO GIVE ... CHEERFULLY

Another person's requests for a loving response from you may come in many forms. Not all of them are pretty and some may make you very uncomfortable. I have worked with adolescents who were so angry and void of love that they threatened my life. Yet love is what they needed and were requesting.

Even when somebody you care deeply about requests a loving response, you may be tempted to come up with many reasons why you can't, don't want to, or shouldn't involve yourself. Maybe you think they deserve your anger more than your love because of something they did.

Most of the reasons to withhold love are based on the fearful voice in your mind that keeps score. "Let's see, I have done nice things for you for three nights, now you have to do something for me." This type of conditional giving is little more than a business transaction, and has nothing to do with expanding your happiness. True giving is not a tidy business transaction where you give with the expectation of something in return from the person.

The ego's law is: When you do something for someone else, be sure you get something back. If you don't, stop giving.

Attitudinal Healing recognizes the law of love: Give love unconditionally and your life will be transformed.

Acting from love will open doors you never imagined were there, as the following story illustrates. When I asked the director of the Austin Center for Attitudinal Healing, Doug Mullins, how he ended up doing the work he was doing he said, "I was living in Colorado, making a fantastic living in computers. I had moved from Texas many years previously. I loved Colorado, and had vowed when I left Texas that I would not return. Colorado was exactly where I wanted to be. Then my daughter, who I had not always had the best relationship with, came to me and asked if I would move to Texas so she could finish school there. It was the last thing I wanted. But when she asked, something inside of me said I needed to do it. I knew it was the voice of love. After being in Texas for a while, the Center ended up needing a director. The Center was a hair away from having to close, and stop serving the hundreds of people it had reached. Here I am, and I know I am in the right place. If I had not honored my daughter's request, I would not be here."

I am not suggesting that one should never say "no." Certainly, having good boundaries is important. However, fear of giving is epidemic in western culture. Generally, people are too focused on what they are going to get from life, rather than what they can give. The result of focusing on "getting" is depression, anger and isolation, not to mention environmental disaster. Attitudinal Healing guides you to the opportunity to heal through extending love, kindness and compassion.

In order to experience how giving and receiving are the same, for one week stop focusing on "getting." Stop making sure that you get your share back. Stop worrying about what you will miss or lose if you give freely. For one week respond to everything you can with love. Give some of your time. Offer acceptance and understanding. Listen to people. This type of service will teach you that giving and receiving are the same.

Unconditional love wants to give itself freely.
Fear-based giving always wants a
return on the investment.

Are You Giving
What You Want for Yourself?

There are many myths about happiness. Most of them are based on the belief that if you are not feeling happy it's because you have not found the right place to live, the right job, or the right mate.

There are essentially three ways your mind will tell you to achieve happiness. They are named for their central characteristic. Only one of them will work, but the good news is that it is never too late to change.

PANHANDLING:

This way of thinking says, "Your heart is empty, so sit and wait for some 'spare love' to come your way." Those in this pattern of thinking tend to come from a background where they either have not had much support, or have been heavily criticized. It is easy for them to live a life where possibilities are never seen, let alone realized. Because they are afraid to love, they wait with their hand outstretched for something in life to be given to them by people they perceive as having more. They tend to feel that the world happens to them and they are just along for the ride. If things are going well, they consider themselves lucky. If things are going bad, they feel like a victim, blaming other people, circumstances, or God.

SEEKING AND CHASING:

This way of thinking says, "Your heart is empty, but there is so much out there that could fill it. Go get some." Here the emphasis is upon looking for something or someone to make you happy. These individuals may have taken the essential step of asking themselves what they want, and may appear active and assertive in creating what they want, but they end up disillusioned time and time again. They are encouraged by a culture which believes the same thing they do, so it is difficult for them to see the insanity. At most, they have fleeting periods of happiness because if they experience suffering they always look to something else on the horizon—a habit which is precisely the cause of the suffering.

GIVING AND RECEIVING:

This way of thinking says, "God's love is in you now. To know it, give it," reflecting the universal truth that giving and receiving are the same. These individuals have not only asked themselves what they want, they have also recognized that what brings happiness, can only increase by giving love away. This takes the focus off of material accumulation and external recognition and onto such traits as love, understanding, patience, tolerance, gentleness and compassion. This way of thinking knows there is nothing constructive in sitting and lamenting about not having what you want. Give what you want for yourself and receive the same.

In actuality there are five steps you can follow to increase your happiness:

    1. Identify the ways you have believed you would achieve happiness.

    2. With honesty and clarity, decide if these beliefs are accurate.

    3. If they are not, determine to let go of them.

    4. Decide what really will result in your happiness.

    5. Start doing this.

These steps sound almost too simple to even bother saying. Yet many people keep doing the same things even though happiness never comes. Practicing Attitudinal Healing can help you stop creating suffering for yourself when you think you are striving for happiness.

The only productive use of time is to give what you truly want for yourself.

"Another word for quiet is 'now.'"

HUGH PRATHER

We can let go
of the past
and of the future.

Add a Little Now to Your Later

You have likely heard the importance of setting and achieving goals countless times. For right now, forget about it. Setting goals for the future may be important, but it is nowhere near as important as learning to be present.

Sometimes the real go-getters become anxious at the suggestion of letting go of goals, even for a moment. Don't worry, future-oriented goals are certainly not all negative. Yet if they are your whole life and you always go from one goal to the next, you are not going to find consistent happiness.

By now you are seeing that focusing on the moment is a central point of Attitudinal Healing. Without it, your happiness will always be fleeting. To get an idea of where you stand in being present, get out a piece of paper and divide it into three columns; past, now and future. Contemplate your life and what you spend your time thinking about. Then place in the three columns the percentage of time that you spend in each. If you are like most people, you will discover that you spend far more time holding onto grudges or guilt about the past, and worrying or trying to control the future, than you do living in the present. With awareness and intention this can change.

On this morning's news, I saw a physician/mountaineer who was caught in a severe storm a few years ago on Mount Everest. Most of his party died. He lost his nose and hands due to frostbite. On the news he was describing how he had been well on his way toward achieving his goal of ascending the great mountain peaks of the world. To his surprise, it was through his failure on Everest that he learned his most important lesson. He acknowledged how he had been so goal-oriented that he overlooked his heart, his love for his family and who he was. Though he lost the hands that had helped him reach his goals, he discovered the heart that delivered him home. "I would never trade them back," he said, his voice trembling with emotion.

To bring a little now to your later, you will need to have strong intentions. This is because your mind is accustomed to obsessing on the past and the future. To break the habit, and bring your mind home to peace, a daily discipline is necessary. If you just leave your mind to go where it will, it will undoubtedly continue to be preoccupied with the past and future, and you will literally put off being happy.

Here is an alternative. In the morning, before your feet hit the floor, establish spiritually-based goals that can be accomplished in the moment throughout the day. These goals will bring balance to your life and any future-oriented goals you may have. Examples of these peace-ensuring goals are:

> *My goal is to listen with my heart today.*
> *My goal is to extend kindness to all I meet.*
> *My goal is to forgive rather than judge.*
> *My goal is to give Love.*

The following is a five-step meditation you can do each day to focus on creating peace-ensuring goals. I suggest you practice it each morning when you wake. It is easy to remember because it is an acronym for PEACE. Thus I call it the **PEACE** Plan.

Picture how you want to feel today and the thoughts you want to have in your mind.

Notice I didn't say "what you want to have happen," for this is often out of your control. But what you think and feel in reaction to external circumstances is completely up to you. This may be hard to see right now, but it is true. It is also the key to your happiness.

Expect that you will think these thoughts and feel this way.

This step uproots the common habit of saying, "Yeah, but if some thing happens that I don't like, I will have every reason to be angry and upset." Today escape this pattern of giving up your happiness by knowing that you alone choose your thoughts and feelings.

Ask, "What is my peace-ensuring goal for the day?"

Peace-ensuring goals are ones that can be accomplished in the moment and result in you being peaceful and happy.

Choose to listen to the gentle voice within you as it offers you your answer.

Enjoy your day and share your peace-ensuring goal with at least one other person.

By practicing peace-ensuring goals
you will add a little now to your later,
and a smile to your life.

FEAR DEPLETES, LOVE ENLIVENS

It seems that in today's world everybody wants more energy. Millions use caffeine, even amphetamines and cocaine. News of the latest food, supplement, or exercise that increases energy fills the tabloids.

If you want real and complete energy, all you need to learn about is love.

In 1981, I spent a few days traveling across India by car with Mother Teresa, stopping in many locations each day. There was not much time for rest other than a brief nod-off in the back seat (please, no jokes about sleeping with Mother Teresa). The schedule was fast paced, and the conditions of poverty we entered were often extremely difficult. At the time, I was in my twenties and an athlete. She was more than three times my age and in failing health. I was the one exhausted. Later, I realized this was because my response to the poverty and illness I saw was to be overwhelmed and to fear that the relief of suffering of so many was hopeless. Her response was one of compassion and deep love. I believe this was the source of her endless energy.

Most people have absolutely no idea how much energy their fear consumes. Like persistent erosion, your fears eat away at your life even when you're not thinking directly about them—even in your sleep. Eventually you may not even notice what a state of stress and anxiety you are in because you forget what peace feels like. If you are not careful, fear becomes that which motivates you. Fear-based motivation never results in peace.

Most fear comes from projecting a negative past into the future. The good news is that it's possible to let go of the past and the future, and thus experience a renewed sense of energy. The following exercise will help you start.

Write down your three biggest fears—the ones that you rarely, if ever, talk about. Fears like, "I am afraid I will be discovered to be incompetent," or, "I am afraid I will be alone all my life," or "I am afraid to die." Read these aloud to yourself and then say, "My mind made these up. Instead of focusing on these fears, I can choose to love." Next, spend five minutes extending love to the part of you that is so fearful. For example, say to the fear of incompetence, "No matter what mistakes you make, you are loved." To the fear of being alone, say, "God's love is available for you to give and receive right now. You are not alone." To the fear of death, say, "Love is eternal. You have nothing to fear."

The best way to get through your fears is to recognize that the solution is always to love. Practicing this with your fears will give you more and lasting energy than even the best double espresso.

The greatest energy depleter is your fear.
The most powerful energizer is love.

THROW AWAY YOUR SCORE CARD

As much as most people dislike bureaucracy and petty details, it is amazing how much red tape exists in our minds. Sometimes when another person needs your help you might find yourself "reviewing their records" to determine whether you should put yourself out or not. Your internal dialogue might resemble a parole hearing: "One moment, please, while I process your request for release. According to my records, you didn't help me with the dishes last night, you forgot our anniversary two years ago, and you have been more than a little ornery lately. Your overall record is dismal. I am so sorry, your request for kindness and patience is being denied. Try again later when you have improved your score."

Keeping score may make you feel superior, but it will ultimately only lead to bitterness and guilt. Acts of love that are given when somebody has not been a saint are the ones that matter the most. Love and kindness are easy when someone is spreading rose petals in your direction. It's another story when they are spreading manure.

Who hasn't said and done some pretty raunchy stuff? If you ask yourself what you really needed during those times, even though you couldn't say it, was it not love?

When adults or children are acting out in some way, it isn't beneficial to only be critical. This is the reaction they are used to. If you can find it in yourself to approach them compassionately, knowing that they are in need of love, the situation almost always turns the corner. To help with this, imagine yourself acting like they are. How would you feel? What would you most want? Give this to them now. It will be as healing for you as for them.

None of this is to suggest that people should not be held responsible for their behavior. Consequences are often needed. But, remember it is during the tough times that your compassion is most needed. Throw away your score card and be willing to come from the heart. Regardless if the other person's behavior changes you will find yourself more at peace—and isn't that what it's all about?

If you offer compassion
when you receive manure,
you will get roses.

"There is no condition, no circumstance, no problem that love cannot solve ….love, for yourself and others, is always the solution."

NEALE DONALD WALSCH

Now is the only time there is, and each instant is for giving.

HAVE PEACE OF MIND
AS YOUR SINGLE GOAL

In years past, I would accomplish a goal, have a moment of satisfaction, go on to the next goal, and achieve that one, only to repeat the pattern. I became a busy achiever but I wasn't very happy. I had the trappings of success, but the grass was often greener on the other side. Consistent peace of mind eluded me.

Despite being unhappy, I used to think I was successful because I could reach many of the goals that I set. Now it seems crazy to consider myself successful if I am not happy. In fact, I would go so far as to say that the key ingredient to success is happiness.

Some goals can be very important, like making enough money for your kid's education, or eating a healthier diet and exercising more. There are many books and seminars on clarifying, setting, and achieving these types of goals. Yet, many of these approaches miss an important point:

> There is only one goal that ultimately matters, one that is an essential part of all others, one that is available to you at all times—peace of mind.

Having peace of mind in the present moment as your single goal allows you to pursue any future-oriented objectives with a sense of calm.

When you have peace of mind as your single goal you are saying to yourself: "No matter what is happening in my life—no matter what my physical condition, rich or poor, no matter if people don't behave and react to me how I want them to—peace of mind is most important, and is always possible."

Imagine that your thoughts are like a swinging pendulum. Peace of mind is where the pendulum will naturally come to rest when given a chance. Calmness enters your life when you turn your mind toward peace because there is nothing more powerful than responding to your call home.

A key ingredient to happiness is to realize that now is the only time there is and each instant is for giving.

ALL THOUGHTS CREATE

Most people pay more attention to the contents of their refrigerator and their bank account than they do the content of their mind. Yet, in order to be truly happy we must first take responsibility for our thoughts.

Think of responsibility as the "ability to respond." If you're holding onto thoughts about the past, or are preoccupied with thoughts about the future, you limit your ability to respond to what is happening now.

Don't make the mistake of underestimating the power of your thoughts. Even the smallest pebble dropped into a pond sends ripples in all directions. It is the same with your thoughts. Simply put, your thoughts are the cause of your suffering, and they hold your release.

A different job, more free time, a different relationship, a long vacation, a new purchase: These are common solutions to feeling something is amiss in life. Though these changes can be positive, they do nothing to address the real cause of your conflict: your thoughts. External changes alone are like giving a new paint job to car with engine problems. When you are unhappy, get in the habit of looking at the engine (i.e., your thoughts) instead of the paint (i.e., the external world).

Bumper sticker philosophy points to the superficial ways in which we look for happiness:

> *"When the going gets tough, the tough go shopping."*
> *"The one who dies with the most toys wins."*

These sayings are good examples of believing that more will make you happier. Your experience is transformed when you change your thoughts of desire to thoughts of giving in the moment. If you want real happiness, change these sayings to:

> *"When the going gets tough, the tough give."*
> *"The one who dies having forgiven all is already in Heaven."*

Because you may have become accustomed to believing that the external world is the source of your experience, it may initially be difficult to believe that all your thoughts create. For example, it is easy to believe that your emotions are like reflexes and they automatically happen when given certain input from the world. This is not true. The feelings and emotions you experience are your creation.

If you are thinking thoughts that are resentful, are you not creating feelings of anger? If you are thinking thoughts about how unloved you are, are you not creating feelings of loneliness? In contrast, if you are thinking forgiving thoughts, are you not creating feelings of love? To change your life for the better, become aware of your thoughts and decide to become active in directing them toward love and kindness.

REMIND YOURSELF OFTEN:
ALL THOUGHTS CREATE.
THEN DECIDE WHAT IT IS
THAT YOU WANT TO MAKE.

EVERY HOUR
SEND A LOVING THOUGHT

— ◖●◗ —

Consider the action of sending loving thoughts as "happiness insurance." It's free, and even better, you receive dividends from what you give.

I believe that all the wisdom of the worlds spiritual teachings are held in four words: Extend love, receive love. There are a thousand ways to distract yourself from these four words, such as becoming too busy, holding onto the past, or harshly judging others. However, there is always one way to return: Choose to do so.

Imagine the world if every person, no matter what was going on, paused each hour and sent a loving thought. Let it begin with you today.

The means to be happy
is with you every minute:
Send a loving thought.

"When you judge others,
you don't define them, you define
yourself as someone who needs to judge
and compartmentalize people … The highest
spiritual act in life is to see yourself in everyone else
and everyone else in you, to surrender yourself and
see everyone's joy and suffering as your own,
to detach yourself from your ego-need to be
attached to the fruits of your labor, and to
simply see everyone else in the
world as part of you."

DR. WAYNE DYER

We can learn to love
ourselves and others
by forgiving rather
than judging.

DO YOU WANT TO BE ANGRY OR DO YOU WANT TO BE HAPPY?

Ironically, I just spent a good deal of time writing this section when my computer unexpectedly shut down, losing all of my work. After staring in disbelief at my darkened screen my first reaction was anger and blame. My anger was initially directed toward my antiquated computer for not working, and thus ruining my morning. My second reaction was to blame myself—for not saving the information, and for not coughing up the money for an updated computer long ago.

Does this sound like I was happy? Obviously not. But despite what part of my mind wanted me to believe, the real reason I was not happy had nothing to do with the unexpected event.

My unhappiness was due to the thoughts I was having, not the event that occurred. This was good news, because then I could do something about being unhappy.

When something goes "wrong" in life, your first reaction might be similar to mine: anger and blame. I, as well as you, can attest that neither of these will lead to being happy. They may lead to feeling right, dominating or self-righteous, but don't confuse these feelings with happiness.

To be happy, it is important to learn to let go of blame and anger as quickly as possible. This is not to say that you should expect to never experience anger, or that if you do, you have failed on your spiritual path. Rather, the intention is not to be taken by your anger and thus abandon your inherent happiness.

I have been amazed by how many people don't want to let go of anger, even when it is depriving them of living a full life. This is because the fearful part of our minds, our ego, tells us that our anger will keep us safe. The ego states that without anger, we will be taken advantage of, become unmotivated, and appear weak. If you look closely at this belief you will discover it is quite insane. Holding onto anger actually keeps you unhappy, feeling alone and unsafe.

You may protest, "Well, I have every reason to be angry!" From one stand-point, who doesn't have reasons to be angry? It is certainly not difficult to look around this world and find plenty to be very angry about. Many arguments are even about who has the greater reason to be angry. What a waste of time! Would it not make more sense to spend your time arguing for your happiness?

Though you may not realize it, you are always choosing between two ways of perceiving: Looking to the world for reasons to be upset, or looking to your heart, to God, for reasons to be happy. I guarantee you will find what you are looking for.

To quote the Dalai Lama: "The only factor that can give you refuge or protection from the destructive effects of anger and hatred is your practice of tolerance and patience." Try to remember:

Patience and tolerance bring you happiness.
Anger and hatred bring you suffering.

If you find yourself stuck in anger, I suggest taking these three steps.

First, say to yourself, "I don't want this. There is another way." You may want to recognize the suffering your anger has caused you by closing your eyes and picturing yourself during times when you have been very angry. You may also want to recognize the suffering of those who have directly and indirectly received your anger. Don't do this to make yourself feel guilty. Do it to help make your decision to do something different.

Second, ask yourself, "Who am I angry with, and what are the ways they must have suffered in their lives?" Asking this sincerely will allow your heart to open to compassion and your mind to develop patience. You might also ask yourself, "What is my anger and lack of forgiveness costing me?"

Third, ask yourself, "What is human nature, and what is God?" This step is larger, and can also be of benefit during times when you are not angry. I believe that as we do this, we begin to see that humans are inherently loving beings, having been created by a loving and forgiving God. Often, we become lost and forget who we are. Being lost we become fearful, and often find ourselves in endless cycles of attack and defense. The response that will bring us home is not anger and upset, but love and understanding.

It is interesting how, if you are open and willing to release your anger, what first appeared to be wrong in your life can be transformed to a gift. Before my computer went off and I lost my information, I was trying to think of a story to illustrate the choice between anger and being happy. Now I have one.

Look to your heart and find reasons to be happy
instead of looking to the past
and to the world for reasons to be upset.

SCHEDULE *"forgiveness practice sessions"*

Around my house, I can get busy and forget (or procrastinate) to take out the trash. Yesterday morning, I found myself with my foot in the kitchen trash can, trying to stuff just one more old milk carton in, rather than making the trip out to the garbage can. I stepped on one of my kid's old half-empty juice boxes, squirting warm, sticky liquid up the leg of my pants. I had to change clothes, wash my leg, and launder the pants. The two-minute walk to take out the garbage would have been much easier.

Similarly, this stuffing process can happen mentally. I can let negative or old thoughts directed at myself and others pile up, and not take the time to let go of them. If I keep stuffing without letting go, something sticky and smelly (like anger) usually squirts out. Then I have a mess to clean up. The few minutes a day it takes to practice forgiveness makes for a much easier life.

I have found that forgiveness practice sessions greatly help to keep my mind clear of thoughts that don't bring me peace. I suggest that once a day, beginning today, you schedule five-minute forgiveness sessions. During this time your task is to think about the people in your life, including yourself, and to see beyond their behavior and into who they are. Imagine their (or your) behavior is like whitecaps on the surface of the ocean. Look beyond the weather and the waves, and into the depths of the water. Visualize a glimmer of light in their hearts, a gentle smile (which even they may be unaware of). Do the same with yourself. Each session, let this light grow brighter, and the smile wider. Undertaking this practice will make you remarkably lighter and happier. People around you will notice the difference too.

The following will help clarify what to focus on during your practice sessions, as well as the importance of doing them.

> *Forgiveness does not mean that you condone all behaviors, or stop holding others accountable for their actions.*
>
> *Forgiveness does mean that you are willing to look for the light of God in everybody.*
>
> *Forgiveness is a result of seeing yourself and other people in the present moment, absent of the past.*
>
> *Forgiveness is choosing to see the light of God in somebody whom you are tempted to judge.*
>
> *Forgiveness is the foundation for your happiness. Practicing it will change your life completely.*

Forgiveness can be misunderstood. The fearful part of your mind can come up with many reasons not to forgive. Choose not to listen to the unforgiving voice and instead remember:

When you forgive you see the love that is within people, no matter how well hidden by their unbecoming behavior.

SEE BEYOND IMPERFECTION

Some kimonos (Japanese robes) have a design and purpose that is very different from western clothes. Certain robes are very plain on the outside and even have imperfections purposely sewn into them. On the inside, they are intricately beautiful and meticulously crafted. I imagine the purpose of the robe is to remind the wearer that their beauty lies within. Those who see the robe being worn, with only the imperfect outside visible, are reminded to think of the magnificence beneath the exterior—of the robe, the person, and themselves.

If all you see is imperfection—I'm too fat, they're unfair, you're not attractive enough—it is the same as focusing only on the outside of the kimono. There is always the option to shift your focus and see the loveliness of what is in the heart.

Looking to what is on the inside of the kimono, beyond the imperfection, is precisely what forgiveness is. When you are able to look beyond the mistakes and imperfections of people and recognize their magnificence, you have practiced forgiveness.

In reference to forgiveness, I often hear the comment, "My (parent, spouse, etc.) has never really expressed their love for me. We barely talk anymore. Do you think that there is a chance that if I offer them blessings and forgiveness they will change?"

This question points to the belief that, for forgiveness to be worthwhile, the other person needs to change in some way. Instead, look within yourself. Forgiveness is your most powerful tool for healing because with forgiveness you always receive blessings—even if the person's behavior does not change. This is because:

When you behold another with the eyes of love,

you see your own magnificence too.

"Man invented language for his deep need to complain."

LILY TOMLIN

We can become
love finders
rather than
fault finders.

BE JUST A LITTLE KINDER THAN YOU NEED TO BE.

While writing this book someone asked me, "If you could only have one of the vignette titles to live by, which would it be?" Though I think they are all important, what the philosopher Aldous Huxley said at the end of his life moves me. Following a lifetime in pursuit of truth, when asked what was most important, he is reported to have said, "After all the years of studying philosophy it is a bit embarrassing that upon departing this world I have little other advice than, 'Be a little kinder than you need to be.'"

You could put this book down now, never read another word of philosophy, religion, or psychology, and do wonderfully well spiritually by living the truth contained in Huxley's one sentence.

At the most basic level, the large problems of the world have one simple solution. What is the answer to prejudice? Kindness. To environmental problems? Kindness. To problems or misunderstanding in your family? Kindness.

Imagine your life if you were a little kinder at home, with people at work, and with strangers. I am not talking about acts that require any sacrifice at all: Perhaps smile at the clerk who seems to be having a bad day. Spend a few minutes of listening to your children with an attitude that they are the most incredible beings you have ever experienced. Give a few dollars or a few hours to a charity.

Kindness comes naturally when you direct your thoughts to recognize how important it is. Your mind can be like fertile land that has been ignored. Before you can expect anything beautiful to grow, you need to cultivate it lovingly. The following are some "cultivating thoughts" that will lead your mind and actions toward kindness:

> The heart of everyone you meet is deserving of kindness.
>
> Holding on to anger and resentments will not bring you what you want.
>
> Withholding kindness is a decision to suffer.
>
> It is to your benefit to be kind.
>
> Nothing good comes from punishing yourself.
>
> Kindness leads to happiness. You deserve to be happy.
>
> The hardest time to be kind is when you feel attacked. It is also the most important. See people who are attacking as fearful, and in need of love.
>
> It is easier to be kind when you focus on a person's heart rather than their behavior.
>
> Everyone, including you, has an innocent child living in them who deserves your kindness.

It is easier to be kind when you focus on your blessings, rather than your hurts.

Judgments are roadblocks to kindness.

Patience is the doorway to kindness.

Your thoughts are like a boomerang. Your judgments and unforgiving thoughts will most certainly return and whack you in the back of the head. Instead:

Make the decision to extend kindness and feel the warmth of love replace everything else.

GIVE YOURSELF THE GIFT
OF QUIET TIME

When a pond is stirred up, the water becomes murky. If allowed to sit still, clarity will gradually return as the sediment settles. The same is true with your mind. Without giving yourself times of stillness and quiet on a regular basis, your mind will not be clear and your decisions and perceptions will be clouded.

A corporate executive I was working with was telling me how she was able to do many things at once, and how this skill is what had saved her many times. I commented to her that, though this is a useful trait some of the time, if you are always in this mode, there is something wrong with the picture. I suggested to her that being able to do nothing and be still is equally, if not more, important.

People who are too busy, over-stressed, and take no time for stillness tend to become fault finders. They always see what is wrong. People who take time for quiet reflection tend to be more able to see through loving eyes.

If you buy into the overemphasis on materialism and achievement in our culture, you will be led to a life of spiritual deprivation. A balance between accomplishment and awareness of the more subtle parts of life—your own heartbeat, the sound of the wind, children playing—is the indicator of a healthy life.

Most people don't have this important balance as they grow up. The majority of schools are task-oriented, and few teach how to have a still mind. Few families emphasize stillness with their busy schedules. I grew up in a family where our appearance to the world was very important. Much of the time, there was more emphasis on what I was doing than on who I was. In other words, doing was more important than being. It was not until a few years after receiving my doctorate in my early twenties that I began to see that I had become very good at accomplishing tasks, but did not know much about being still. During the last twenty-five years, I have continued to see the value of quiet time each day. However, quiet time does not always come easy. There have been many times when I have created the space for still reflection, only to fill up that space with tasks that seem all too important at the time. I have come to see that, each year, I do a little better at maintaining uninterrupted space, and for this I am grateful. And when my tricky mind sneaks its "to do" list into my quiet space, I try and have a sense of humor about it, as though I am training a puppy who has a very short attention span.

There are two types of quiet time that are important. One was described above, and can be built into your day: Perhaps fifteen minutes in the morning and evening for meditation, contemplation and prayer. The other, described below, is learning to pause when you are upset.

When you are having a bad day, you probably don't realize that you have made a choice. Even though your reactions may feel automatic, there is always a thought behind them. In order to recognize these thoughts and be able to do something different, be willing to pause and reflect. Most of the time when people are having a bad day, they do things and think thoughts that are the equivalent of throwing fuel on flames. Instead, learn to use any upset as a cue for you to pause. Tell yourself, "There is another way to see this. I am not a robot, and I don't have to react in any particular way."

Don't fool yourself into thinking that when you are upset you should always do something. If you are honest with yourself, probably your worst decisions and actions have come from being upset. The best course of action when you are upset is to take time to pause and be still, before you respond.

When it comes to taking quiet time, most people have the tendency to procrastinate, seeing other tasks as more important. Don't. Your peace of mind depends on it.

Having time each day for being still
is a prerequisite for peace of mind
and clarity of vision.

KNOW WHAT YOU CAN CHANGE
AND WHAT YOU CAN'T

— ◀ ● ▶ —

Remember as a kid when you were asked, "If a genie gave you only one wish, what would it be?" You probably were not very old before you learned to quickly answer, "A million more wishes!"

Here is a similar question: "If you could change just one thing, what would it be?"

The answer that is equivalent to "a million more wishes" is, "My thoughts!" When you learn to look to your thoughts whenever you are upset in any way, you have discovered true freedom, even beyond the genie's million wishes. You can always choose to redirect your thoughts.

Though the world isn't responsible for how you feel, you do have a part in creating outcomes. Most fault finding is done after something happens that you don't like. This is like going to a restaurant, demanding food without reading the menu, and then complaining about the food that is brought to you. Instead of saying, "Wow, I guess I should have thought about what I wanted," you blame the waitperson, the cook, and the establishment rather than seeing your part in the fiasco.

Have you ever been asked what you want in a situation, and replied, "I'm not sure what I want to happen, but I sure know what I don't want." This is your ego speaking and showing its true colors. It only focuses on the negative, and has no idea about any positive outcome. The time to think about what you want to happen is at the beginning. Don't wait until the waitperson brings you the food and then complain. Ask yourself at the beginning of any situation that you are uncertain about, "What do I want to have happen?" Even more importantly, ask yourself, "What is the purpose of this situation?"

I worked with a man who was in a sales position. He was making excellent money, but was extremely stressed out. Every time he didn't make a sale he felt the weight of the world on his shoulders. I asked him to ponder this question, prior to each sales call: "What is the real purpose of this interaction?" To his surprise, his answers had nothing to do with making a sale! His answers kept being things like, "Be genuinely interested in this person." "Be patient and kind." "See their heart." His smile during his meetings changed from a fake one, worn by an over-stressed salesman, to a genuine one of a fellow human being. Not only did his stress disappear, his sales went up! Of course they did. Who would you rather be in a relationship with, business or personal—somebody who only wanted something from you, or somebody who clearly cared about you?

When you put a positive goal at the beginning of any situation it will determine the outcome. The ego does the opposite by going into a situation with no positive goal. It proceeds to find fault in whatever is going on, and then blames other people or circumstances when the outcome is something it deems less than satisfactory. Don't spend your life in this cycle of insanity! Stop looking back at what happened, feeling short-changed, or trying to figure out what went wrong. Instead, put your undivided attention on placing positive goals at the beginning—goals that are not based on the external but that have to do with your perception and personal actions. When you do this, you will acquire the ability to focus on the positive aspects (love finding) of a situation by overlooking any obstacles (fault finding) that get in your way.

Fault finding comes from believing your happiness comes from the world going according to your liking.

"Faced with a crisis that demands resolution ...
you need to search for the potential for
spiritual growth inherent in the situation."

CAROLINE MYSS, PH.D.

We can choose and direct ourselves to be peaceful inside regardless of what is happening outside.

QUIT SAYING, *"What else can go wrong?"*

Have you ever noticed a tendency that, when your day doesn't go as well as planned, you might say, "What else can go wrong?" Yet, in response to positive occurrences you tend to say, "Boy, that'll never happen again." This is because your ego expects negative circumstances to follow negative circumstances, but believes you're just lucky if something positive happens.

To get an idea of how your thoughts create positive or negative responses, imagine yourself at the top of a snow-covered hill and you have just made a snowball about three feet in diameter. You give your ball a push, and down the hill it travels, picking up speed and size on its own. None of this would surprise you, of course, for you understand the nature of gravity. You also know that snowballs tend to get larger when they are rolled because snow sticks to itself.

Your mind works in a very similar manner. When you have a thought, and you give it a little energy, it will pick up momentum. Like the snowball, once your thought is on a roll it will take up more of your consciousness by attracting like-minded thinking. Negative thoughts stick to other negative thoughts. Let's say, for example, you are having an okay day. Suddenly your boss walks in, appearing to be having a bad day. She begins to point out whatever she thinks you are doing wrong, and then gives you a "priority project." After your boss leaves, you realize that you forgot your lunch and, with the extra work, you don't have time to go out today. You mutter under your breath, "What else can possibly go wrong?" Next, though you might not realize it, you begin looking for what is going to further mess up your day. Your mood goes sour, and maybe you even become a little like your boss was earlier, having a negative attitude with other people. This, in turn, gives you unwanted responses from your co-workers, which gives you all the more reason to continue your "bad day."

Your "bad day" didn't get started because of your surly boss or because you missed lunch. It happened because you had a thought that you gave a little shove at the top of a hill, and down it went, getting bigger with like-minded negative thoughts.

The good news is that once you begin to see this, there are a couple of ways to stop it. First, imagine you are back at the top of the snow-covered hill. This time, you notice there are two piles of snow to make your snowballs from. One is slightly dark, with a dingy appearance. The other is glistening white and sparkling in the sun. Over the dingy pile is the phrase, "Past pain and fear." Over the shimmering pile is the phrase, "Present joy and love." Imagine that the hill is your mind. Which snowballs do you want to send down it, growing along the way?

Second, if you overlooked your choice at the top of the hill and find that your negative thinking is already on a pretty good roll, imagine that you can get out in front of your dingy snowball-thinking and yell, "Stop!" It does. Of course it stops! The original thought was your creation. You gave it the energy to get it going. When you withdraw your energy from it, it ceases to exist.

What this is saying is that:

- You have control over your response to circumstances.

- When you look for what is wrong, you will find it.

- When you look for what is positive, you will find it.

- What you put energy into creates momentum.

- You can stop your negative thinking by choosing to do so.

- You should choose your piles of snow carefully.

Train your mind to be on the lookout for the positive.

When good things happen say,
"WHAT ELSE IS GOING TO
GO **RIGHT** TODAY?"

COMPLIMENT MORE THAN YOU COMPLAIN OR CRITICIZE

Your mind comes equipped with a magnifying glass that, though you may not realize it, you use every day. This magnifying glass can bring you great joy or constant conflict, depending on your focus.

When you negatively criticize another person (or yourself) you are not seeing who they are. You are putting a magnifying glass up to mistakes instead of looking beyond them. This leads to experiencing anger, resentment and conflict.

Change your focus and change your life! It is that simple. Choose to hold your magnifying glass up to the heart and you will see love. Remove your focus from mistakes and errors, and you will experience the peace that comes from allowing love to exist as it is, always has been, and always will be.

Do you remember, as a kid, looking into a microscope for the first time? An entire new world came into view, a world that you never before knew existed. When you choose to magnify the heart you will have the same amazement as when you first gazed into a microscope.

As you magnify love, you will discover plenty to compliment. In contrast, if you magnify mistakes, you will find plenty to criticize or complain about. Where you put your focus is up to you.

To magnify the heart, it is important, at least for a brief interval, to let go of your future goals and your past mistakes. To have peace of mind, use your mind's magnifying glass to look for innocence in the present moment.

Imagine that even somebody who has done things which you find very difficult to forgive has a place within him or her that is unmarred by any past actions—maybe just a speck of light. If you have a lot of anger for this person (who may even be you) imagine that this spot of love is as small as a single cell, but it is most definitely there. Now, pull out your incredibly strong magnifying glass. Focus on this single cell of love and let it be all you look at for a time.

All of us have a choice of what to magnify: anger and fear, or forgiveness and love. When you find yourself upset in any way, it is helpful to remind yourself that you are magnifying something other than the heart. During these difficult times say to yourself, "I don't want to magnify my anger, criticism or complaints. I want to magnify love and innocence."

This thought will keep you safe in a world where there seems to be endless obstacles to focusing on love. No matter what happens during your day, you can respond with this one thought and release yourself from all pain and misery.

Sometimes when I suggest this to people, they look at me like I am living in a fantasy world. Nothing is further from the truth. In fact, when I'm not seeing love is when I am living in illusion. By focusing on love, you are looking for something that is most definitely there. The goal isn't to pretend to see something that does not exist; it is to train your mind to look beyond the mistakes so you can see what is really there.

Rather than looking forward or back in time, look directly into the present.

How to find love:
Look past your criticisms and complaints
and straight into the heart.

GET RID OF YOUR "YEAH, BUTS"

Many individuals throw away their peace of mind for reasons as small as a traffic jam. Resist coming up with ways by which your happiness and peace of mind can be taken away, or reasons you can't have it in the first place. Every time you have a thought like, "Well, maybe I can have peace of mind now, but if I lost my job I couldn't," you are giving up your peace of mind.

Last weekend, a septic line broke at my home, quickly filling my back yard with … well, I'll spare you the details. Though I can procrastinate with the best of them when it comes to home repair, I immediately called the repair people. A broken septic line is not something one puts off by saying, "Well, I have some other things to do first, I'll get to it later." On the contrary, nothing in the universe was going to take precedence over getting the flow of sewage in my back yard to stop.

Peace of mind needs to be dealt with in the same manner as a broken septic line. If I had the same commitment to peace of mind that I had to a broken septic line, I would likely be quite an enlightened soul. Nothing can be more important in any given moment than peace of mind.

During the 1998 International Conference for Attitudinal Healing, I met a most remarkable woman by the name of Pilar. Her eyes were as full of light as any I have ever seen. I learned that this was not always the case. Pilar was born with no arms and a deformed body. She believed for most of her life that she was a victim. She was angry with her mother, furious with life, and very distant from God. Consequently, she did very little with her life. Pilar felt that most people just stared at her body and wanted nothing to do with her. She felt isolated in a cruel, harsh world.

Pilar first discovered Attitudinal Healing in her home of Argentina. She was so lifted by the principles that she decided she had something to offer the world and wanted to become an artist. This made little sense to anyone, because she has no hands or arms. Nonetheless she went to college and finished with a degree in art.

Today, Pilar is a very famous artist, creating intricate and beautiful paintings using her feet. She loves life and is truly an inspiration to us all to get rid of any statements that begin with, "I could be happy, but …"

Take a look at your own "yeah, buts." Remind yourself that happiness and a fulfilling life are always possible when you forgive and follow your dreams.

Painful circumstances may be unavoidable
but suffering is optional.

"Learning is finding out what you already know.
Doing is demonstrating that you know it.
Teaching is reminding others that they know
it just as well as you. You are
all learners, doers, teachers."

RICHARD BACH

We are students
and teachers to
each other.

Throw Away Your Measuring Stick

Toddlers play with such presence and truth. They smile and laugh, and when hurt, they cry and want to be held. Such simplicity. Such purity.

Tragically, in most instances, our culture begins to teach children very early to compare themselves to others in order to figure out not only how they are doing, but also who they are. Grades are given in school, teams are picked in sports and somebody needs to be chosen last, the "in" groups are formed.

By teenage years, models and movie stars become the standard for how we should look. Categories are created which we then use to label others and ourselves: rich and poor, smart and dumb, attractive and ugly. Innocence is lost. The message is given, "Be concerned with how you look, what you have, and what you do." For many, it never stops. Some fret with trying to figure out who they are through comparison until the very end of life, wanting to have just the right funeral—at least better than Uncle Phil's.

Attitudinal Healing recognizes that true self-esteem is never achieved by comparing yourself to others. At best, this form of comparison results in feeling superior. At worst, in feeling weak, ineffectual, powerless—a failure.

The fool's gold of the ego is believing that feelings of superiority are self-esteem. Nothing is farther from the truth. The compulsive need to always be the best comes from fear and low self-worth. In contrast, knowing who you are, and recognizing that another person's loss is not your gain, brings peace to your mind and love to other beings. This is true security.

An initial step in discovering yourself and realizing your connection with God is to stop asking, "How do I measure up?" Once you do this, you will start realizing we are all teachers and students to one another.

Comparison may lead to feelings of superiority, or pervasive feelings of not being good enough. Either way, comparison will eventually result in feelings of being separate and alone. This is because when we compare, we are coming from fear and are looking for outside measurements to figure out who we are.

In contrast, when we look to others as our teachers in learning to love, we experience the peace of God. A main aspect of being on a spiritual path is seeing that we are all teachers and students to each other.

By throwing away your measuring stick
you begin to be able to look
into your heart and to God.
This is how you will know who you are.

DON'T TRY TO MAKE A ROUND PEG FIT INTO A SQUARE HOLE

————— ◄●► —————

Sometimes, without even realizing it, I have tried to make other people be who I want them to be. When I do this, I am denying that they are my teachers.

I have also tried to make myself be somebody that I am not. I did this in hopes of making someone else happy or of getting approval. In the process, I overlooked how we could learn from each other.

It is now clear to me that if I want to be happy and have close relationships, I must begin by seeing and respecting myself and other people for who we are. Seeing us all as students and teachers to each other transforms even the most difficult relationships into classrooms in which we learn the lessons of love.

I once heard the author Ram Dass tell a story that, over time, changed how I related to people. The story was about his relationship with his brother, who was severely mentally ill. As I recall, Ram Dass would visit his brother, but would eventually become frustrated with his lack of response. His brother was clearly "in another world" and could not, or would not, connect with anybody in "this world." In order to be more peaceful, Ram Dass tried meditating before and during his visits. Nothing seemed to work. Understandably, over time, his visits became less frequent and more frustrating. One day, Ram Dass realized he was trying to make his brother enter "the world of Ram Dass" and relate according to his rules. Eventually, Ram Dass was guided to do something different … he entered his brother's world. In doing so, he had to suspend judgment. As you might imagine, everything changed. In these visits, Ram Dass stopped trying to make his brother be somebody he was not. He had a willingness to do his best to meet his brother where he was, without judgment and expectations. The result was a wonderful bonding.

If you want to have close relationships:

- Give up trying to make people live by your agenda.
- Try to get to know others by gaining an understanding of their world.
- Have a willingness to suspend judgment and expectations.
- See them as your teacher in opening your heart.

Another reminder of not trying to make a round peg fit into a square hole came today. As I was writing the story of Ram Dass, a case of my books arrived from the publisher. They were dropped at the top of my driveway by a delivery service. As I saw my dog Simba walk in that general direction, I ran outside—because I know Simba! I was too late to stop it, but right on time to see Simba lift his leg with what seemed to be deliberate aim. "Simba!" I yelled, as he looked back with surprise. He walked up to me as if to say, "Hey, I'm just doing what it is that I do. I'm a guy dog and guy dogs pee on anything new in the yard." He then walked away, wagging his tail—clearly joyful that he was who he was.

My whole life, animals have been my teachers. I often think my dogs are more spiritually advanced than I am! They basically live to offer unconditional affection, chase an occasional cat, wag their tails whenever my kids come down the drive-way, and get a little wild under the full moon. They never try to make me into somebody I am not. In fact, they seem to know what is best about me even when I have forgotten.

In short, they appear to practice something we can all learn from:

Know what matters and don't be bothered with the rest.

How to Get Rid of All Your Enemies: Turn Them into Teachers

———— ◄ ● ► ————

There was once a fellow who saw everyone around him as his enemy. His view was that his kids gave him nothing but problems, his wife was constantly cross with him, the people he worked with were a bunch of morons, and the government was even worse. He constantly complained that just about every person around him seemed to be out to get him. Finally he began praying to have a different life—day after day, week after week, and year after year. Eventually, even God became his enemy, for why would a loving God give him such a miserable life and never answer his prayers? After he died he was complaining once again to God. Finally God said, "My son, you kept praying for a different life and I kept sending you teachers to teach you what you needed to be happy. I sent you your children to teach you understanding, patience and perseverance. I sent you your wife to teach you how to listen with the heart. I sent you countless people to teach you how to forgive, and even more to teach you how to be of service and make a difference. In your next life, please pay attention to the teachers I send you and it will go much more smoothly than this last time around."

Think what it would be like to get up in the morning and know that the world was full of your teachers. Not one enemy, only people to help you along on your spiritual path. The guy who cuts you off on the freeway is there to teach you about letting go. The person who is late for your appointment is there to teach you about patience. Your spouse is there to teach you about kindness. Literally everyone who comes into your life is there to teach you how to see from the perspective of love and respond in compassion.

There have been times when I have tried to avoid the following spiritual truth: Often the people who you become the most angry with are the people who have the most to teach you. I have had resistance to this because my ego finds it much easier to be self-righteous, superior and right, than to be humble and look to all as my teachers.

If you really are honest with yourself, you probably get most upset at people for one of two reasons:
  1. You see something in them you don't want to look at in yourself.
  2. They are here to teach you a skill that you really need to learn
      but don't want to.

For example, if somebody in your life has been dishonest with you, perhaps they are here to remind you to look at the small ways in which you are dishonest. They become your teacher in forgiveness and the development of integrity.

One of the most important perceptual shifts you can make is to stop seeing enemies and start seeing teachers. This will not only allow you to be more peaceful, it will lead you to being more of the person you want to be.

When you stop seeing enemies and
start seeing teachers, all people of the world
become reflections of God. Kindness and
gratitude become your response to all.

"I know not with what weapons World War III will be fought,
but World War IV will be fought with sticks and stones."

ALBERT EINSTEIN

We can focus
on the whole of
life rather than
the fragments.

RIGID BRANCHES BREAK
IN THE FIRST WIND

———— ❬ ◉ ❭ ————

Have you ever noticed which branches of a tree are the first to break in a strong wind? The branches that are supple and able to bend with the wind are able to survive, while those that are rigid snap, though often they appear the strongest.

How you respond to stress and change is imperative to your peace of mind. Despite how strong you might appear, if you are unwilling to listen, compromise, or change, you will likely be doing a great deal of "snapping." In contrast, being able to bend in the inevitable winds of life leads to calm and happiness.

You become stiff and inflexible by having narrow vision, a closed mind, and focusing on the little, fragmented pieces of life. The more you do this the more you lose the ability to see from a larger and more peaceful perspective.

The ego's faulty logic tells you that if you take care of all the little stuff you will be less stressed. When you feel overwhelmed, this approach can make sense. The problem is that the more you focus upon the little stuff, ignoring the larger truths to life, the higher your stress level goes. This does not mean to just ignore all the details and problems of your life and try to be blissful. Rather, don't overlook God and the whole of your life as you go about your daily activities.

The ego wants to solve problems by separating everything into little pieces: money, relationship, work, family. In the process, it forgets about the whole and the higher purposes of life—such as giving and receiving love.

There is an old story of two blind men describing an elephant. One is feeling the tail, the other the trunk. Neither of them describes the entire elephant, believing instead that their little piece is the whole animal. Similarly, it is easy to miss the meaning of your life when you focus on the small fragments.

The five most common ways of focusing on the fragments are by becoming overly concerned with:

1. What somebody did or said in the past.
2. Lack of reciprocation.
3. Mistakes.
4. Your body.
5. Money.

Think about how much time you spend on these concerns. They have no ability in themselves to determine your happiness—it is only your over-focusing upon them that deprives you of peace.

If you step back and remind yourself that there is something beyond the fragments, your stress will begin to dissipate, automatically and immediately. This is because as you broaden your focus you will see the whole of life, which is always love.

When I am upset about something, one question that helps me to step back is, "Will this matter to me five years from now?" To fully answer the question I have to broaden my vision, focus on the whole, and thus recognize what is really important.

There are ways of directing your mind that will lead you to seeing the whole. I call these "Doorways to Truth." The five primary doorways are:

1. Look for love in the present moment.
2. Know all minds are joined and want love.
3. Forgive.
4. See opportunities to learn in all circumstances.
5. Recognize the abundance of all that is important.

The narrow-thinking mind hides the power of all you are from your awareness.

KNOW WHAT'S ENOUGH

You are, no doubt, quite familiar with the nagging voice in your head that keeps the pressure on by saying things like: "Take on more. Accomplish more. Get more done in less time. Make more money. Buy more and better possessions."

Of all the things you can know, knowing what is enough is one of the most important. This knowledge is the core of a simple life. It comes from looking at the whole of life rather than the fragments. In contrast, always wanting more, bigger, and better will take you on an endless and relentless treadmill, leading you away from the simple knowledge of what is enough. In the process of accomplishing and acquiring, without asking yourself what is enough, you lose sight of what is important.

Until you learn to recognize what is enough, nothing will give you true or lasting satisfaction. When you are on the treadmill, you will likely delude yourself into thinking that you will soon have time for what is important. But the time never comes because you don't ask yourself three words, "What is enough?"

You have probably bought items of technology believing they would give you more time for what is important. Did fax machines give you more time at home? Did e-mail give you more time to yourself for contemplation? Did the Internet offer you extra free time? Of course this is not the fault of technology, rather it is a result of your thinking. Technology, like anything else, can be a tool to free you or imprison you. If you have a "take on more" mentality, you will find ways to take on more. If you have a "know what is enough" focus, you will have time in your life for what is important. With this you will use technology and other means to support you in having enough.

Pay attention to what is enough
by looking to the whole of life.
This is essentially what spirituality is,
and it is the source of simplicity.

Watch Your Language

—— ◄ ● ► ——

In 1984, while living in Mexico, I attended a language school. In the process of learning a new vocabulary, I became aware of the words that limit happiness, negatively judge, or label. I found that I had the unique opportunity to choose to not learn certain words.

Simply put, words can help set you free or keep you stuck in unhappiness. More specifically:

Language is the structure of your thoughts.
Your thoughts create your experience.
Therefore, the words you use can shape your life.

"Limiting words" are ones which describe you or another person as anything other than a spiritual being in a limitless moment—words such as can't, impossible, and never. "Judging words" are ones which keep unforgiving thoughts going—words such as inferior, stupid and weak. "Labeling words" are ones which categorize or pigeonhole in a way that holds an individual or group back from all they can be—words such as hopeless, useless, or any words used in a racist manner.

When you choose to stop using words which limit, judge or label, your life becomes more peaceful. Without the negative words, it is hard to have the negative thoughts, and in their place you discover more compassionate and loving thoughts. I like to think of this as "word surgery." If there were something toxic in your body, surely you would want it removed to allow the body to flourish in its state of health. Similarly, by not using limiting, judging or labeling words, you allow your mind to return to its natural state of love. If these words do come up in your thinking, try to stop and see that you must be entertaining a false belief about yourself or another person, and your thinking has become toxic. Remove the words and allow your mind to return to love.

Try the following ten-minute experiment to demonstrate the power of words. In the first five minutes repeat the following five words to yourself:

Hate, Impossible, Afraid, Frown, Separate.

Note how you feel: Probably pretty yucky. In the next five minutes repeat the following five words to yourself:

Forgive, Possible, Love, Smile, One.

Note how you feel: Probably pretty wonderful! All from just thinking a few words. This gives you good reason to watch your language.

You have surely been asked questions like, "If you could only have one food for the rest of your life, what would it be?" Ask yourself the similar type of question, "If you could only have one word for the rest of your life what would it be?" Mine would be love.

{ *Let love be the source of all your thoughts, all your words, and all your actions.* }

"If you spend your life overly concerned with just the temporary affairs of this lifetime, and make no preparation for it [death], then on the day when it comes you will be unable to think about anything except your own mental suffering and fear, and will have no opportunity to practice anything else."

THE DALAI LAMA

Since love
is eternal,
death need not
be viewed
as fearful.

On their deathbed nobody says, *"Gee, I wish I had spent a little more time at the office."*

───── ❮ ● ❯ ─────

What many people do say on their deathbed is, "I wish I had spent more time loving those around me." It is ironic that we can yearn for what we have available to us at all times. But because of our egos, this can be the case.

Innumerable people spend most of their lives getting things done which seem important, but they lose sight of what is really important. When the end comes, they have regrets. They wish they had lived a more balanced life. A painful discovery is often made through the process of dying: Without love, even the most momentous life achievement is empty. It is no wonder that those who have come close to dying almost always describe it as a positive, life-changing experience. They come out of it with a deep sense of what is important and what doesn't really matter.

If you knew that your time was limited, how would you want to live your life today, this month, and this year? For most of us, the answer includes loving more deeply, expressively, completely and consistently. When we think of our time as limited, our thoughts seem to automatically go to what is important rather than the trivial.

Your time in this life is limited, so begin living your days knowing that each of them is a precious gift. The finite nature of this existence is something that is often overlooked because death is feared. Death is often hidden from view because nobody wants to be reminded of the end.

An alternative to the fear and denial of death is to see that you are here for one purpose—to give and receive love, and that this love is eternal. Tremendous peace comes with the recognition of your purpose, and that love lives beyond the end of your body's existence.

Satisfying work, personal strength, and successful, intimate relationships can be the exception rather than the rule. This is because we have forgotten what their source is. Imagine someone exerting great effort to push a car that has run out of fuel. Despite being right next to a gas station the stranded driver still pushes, complains and struggles. This is the case with many of our lives. We struggle instead of taking the time to pause and give and receive love, even though this is precisely what will make our lives run smoothly.

A love-centered life is certainly not a new idea, but it is a much needed one. Love does not promise a pain-free and trouble-free life, but it does offer one of tremendous peace, depth and meaning. Love is not to be figured out or understood with the mind: It is to be experienced with the heart.

Love now.

There is literally no time like the present.

Don't Wait for the Funeral to Forgive or to Say How You Feel

My father is fond of saying, "If I were to discover a pill that, with absolutely no side affects, would guarantee you peace, reduced stress, better health, close relationships, and increased vitality, it would be a miracle! There is such a miracle, it is called forgiveness!"

When I have suffered in my life, it has been from lack of forgiveness. Similarly, I have witnessed patients grieving the death of somebody whom they had not forgiven. Often, their grief stems from wishing they had communicated a few words like, "I love you."

There is a problem with being so angry at somebody that you want them to take their guilt to the grave: Until you forgive, you carry guilt through your life. You might like to believe that your anger and upset will vanish when somebody dies, but it is not true. It is with your own thoughts that you must work, and it is never too late to practice forgiveness. The opportunity to forgive isn't withdrawn at the time of death.

I have encountered numerous individuals who so wished they had dealt with an unhealed relationship before their own death was upon them. Things look quite different when you know you are soon to depart. Like the first time one flies in an airplane, looking down and seeing how small everything looks, death brings with it the perspective that all the anger and unforgiving thoughts are quite small, trivial and insignificant. It makes sense to strive to see this while you are still alive and kicking.

Many relationships are plagued by a lack of shared feelings. Part of physical, emotional and spiritual health is being able to experience and communicate your feelings. Unfortunately, many people rarely, if ever, communicate how they feel. Countless people develop physical illness from having anger, loneliness, and guilt attack their bodies. Many others never have emotional intimacy because of unexpressed feelings. So much suffering results from not talking honestly from the heart.

Think about the people in your life. If they were not here any longer, or if you were soon to depart, is there something you would have wished you had said or hoped they would have known? Tell them today!

When you see today for all it holds,
and all it doesn't have to,
you start to live.

SPEND AS MUCH TIME WITH NATURE AS YOU DO WITH TECHNOLOGY

With all life's flash and glitz, it is easy to lose appreciation for the ordinary, the simple things in life. Technology has great potential to bring us together, and share, but if you drift too far from the grounding of nature, people, and love you will become lost.

Within the ordinary occurrences of nature, the path to the sacred is found: the scent of pine in the forest; your bare feet upon sun drenched white sand; an expanse of green grass blowing in a summer breeze as you lean back to watch wisps of white clouds dance across the sky; looking out your window to see the stars sparkling across the expanse of the universe.

Time with nature brings balance. Without it, your life path can become shallow, even dangerous. With it, you stay connected to your source.

I would rather see fewer prescriptions for Valium and Prozac and more for turning to nature. Many years ago, I found myself doing well in my career, but I was not feeling a strong sense of purpose or meaning in my life. I backpacked into the Sierra Nevada Mountains, knowing that being in nature was somehow important. After a few days, I discovered a renewed sense of purpose to my life, purely by being close to nature. If you asked me to put my experience in words, I don't think I could—it is more of a feeling, a knowing. Many times in my life I have embarked on similar journeys, sometimes only for a few hours. I have never entered nature with the purpose of finding grounding and balance and come up short.

Too much time away from nature and you forget
that you are part of a quiet rhythm.
Allow nature to soften your soul
and heal your heart.

"I define love thus:
The will to extend one's self for the
purpose of nurturing one's own or another's
spiritual growth…Whenever we do actually
exert ourselves in the cause of spiritual growth,
it is because we have chosen to do so.
The choice to love has been made."

M. SCOTT PECK

We can always perceive
ourselves and others as
either extending love
or giving a call for help.

Patience is
The Greatest Gift You Can Give

I can't think of anything that patience doesn't improve. It is like angels left something for us mortals to use. Every time somebody has been patient with me, there is instant bonding and appreciation in my heart, even if I was not able to show it.

Patience is always an extension of love, and therefore always is of benefit. If some-one is having a difficult time, getting upset, judging, or pressuring may get some type of result, but they will never improve the quality of the relationship. However, if you respond with patience, the situation takes on a different energy and feeling.

The best way to shift a situation from a problematic struggle to a positive communication is to stop judging and see the person as making a call for help—for love. Remember, calls for help are not always straightforward. Sometimes the ugliest of behavior from another person is really a call for help. No matter what they are saying or doing, think of a subtitle flashing across their heart saying, "The reason I am behaving this way is that I feel afraid and alone. What I really want is to be loved."

Although patience is something we give other people, as with all acts of love, we are equal recipients of the gift. Patience directly teaches that to give is to receive. The simplest reason to be patient is that it feels a whole lot better than being a controlling, stressed-out maniac. When you make the choice to develop patience, you take a tremendous weight off of your shoulders. Then your heart naturally opens.

When you become uptight, or try to force something to happen according to your time, it is because you are untrusting of the outcome. This is where a spiritual focus can change your life. For example, if you know that the most important thing to do is to extend love, and you trust in the outcome when love is the guide, then you can wait without anxiety. So, it can be said that to be patient is to trust in the power of love.

Another way of saying this is that you become impatient when you are afraid. You end up trying to control (which you are doing whenever you are not being patient) when you fear that the future won't be how you think it should be, or when you fear the past will repeat itself.

Speed seems to be a hot commodity today. Faster is what sells—faster people, faster computers, and faster travel. If a discussion takes more than a sound bite it seems too long.

In contrast, I have yet to see the word "speed" in conjunction with any true spiritual practice. Something miraculous happens when you decide to be patient. Patience opens the door to the magic of the moment, where lessons of love abound and anything is possible.

Fear and impatience are inseparable. Patient comes when you trust in the power of God's love.

DEVELOP AWARENESS, TRUST YOUR HEART, AND TAKE AN ACTION

Are you busy but without purpose? Are you reluctant to make decisions or changes because you are afraid you will make a mistake or fail? If the answer is "yes" to either question, you are not alone. Many people have a block in the natural cycle of awareness, trust and action.

Though it is typically not difficult for me to make decisions, earlier today I took at least three hours to make a relatively simple one. I made the whole thing into quite a big deal. Instead of paying attention to what I knew to be true, I became way too involved in my head. I weighed the alternatives, I thought of which decision was best for other people, I considered time constraints, I tried to predict the outcome of all alternatives, I prayed (as well as can be done when I am stuck in my intellect), and I talked. I exhausted myself. Finally, I made a decision. Then I changed my mind. At last, I laughed at how far from simple wisdom I can wander.

It is difficult to see the truth about a situation, or to know how to react, when you are wringing out your mind like a wet towel.

In my work with animals, especially herd animals such as horses, I have noticed that they're always aware. There is a sensitivity to their surroundings, to the life in and around them, and to what action is needed. There is absolutely nothing dishonest about them. Their actions come from being aware of, and trusting in, a natural wisdom. They don't say, as I did earlier today, "Well, a part of me feels this way, and part of me feels the other way." Based on their awareness, and trusting in the information that comes from that awareness, they take action. There is no, "Am I making the right decision?" There is no, "I need more information." There is no, "Can you give me more time?"

In response to my observations on the wisdom of animals it has been said to me, "Well, humans have a cerebral cortex that differentiates us from animals. With it, we can think and reason." I reply, "As with any advanced technology, it is good to know how and when to turn the thing off." Reason and other "higher" brain functions can be wonderful tools, but they can also be slippery partners. Sometimes, if not most times, we are way too much in our heads. To make good decisions and take appropriate actions, take time each day to ask yourself the following:

What am I aware of?

Use your five senses, plus be aware of your soul and your connection with all that is.

What am I feeling in my heart?

Many times, the answers of the heart are beyond words, and come via a "sense of knowing." God speaks to you through your heart, but not always in words.

What action(s) am I guided to take?

Here is where you may have to stretch. It is one thing to listen to guidance, but it takes guts to follow it. Change occurs whether you want it or not, so you might as well try following your inner guidance. In doing so, change becomes your friend because you come to know the one aspect of life that never changes: God's love for you.

Be aware of all you are.
Trust who speaks to you through your heart.
Take loving actions,
and know you do not walk alone.

LEARN TO BE WITH YOURSELF

Many people are so busy attending to the details of their life that they don't know how to be with themselves. With so much to do, and with so little time to oneself, spiritual thirst often goes unrecognized for what it is. Depression, anxiety and boredom can be symptoms of an unanswered call to a spiritual path.

I have found the things people say they want the most are: positive relationships, good health, personal power and self-esteem. There is a great deal of time and money spent pursuing them. Unfortunately the most important and natural first step to achieving these is often overlooked—spending reflective time with yourself.

Conflicted relationships, low self-esteem, and lack of peace of mind are all indicators that you need to be spending contemplative time with yourself. Yet, often, people don't do this because they believe they should be spending all their time fixing problems.

You cannot be powerful and be afraid of who you are. When you are afraid, the most you can do is control. Though many have come to believe that this is power, it is not. Authentic power comes from knowing your connection with all that is. When you spend reflective time with yourself you discover this power.

Power is knowing that God loves you. This knowledge will change your whole world. That is not to say that knowing yourself and your connection with God releases you from the challenges and pains of living, but it does give you an anchor and a compass during the storms. The anchor is faith and the compass is hope.

Hope and faith help us to envision a positive outcome, even during trying times. I know of nobody with strong hope and faith who does not spend time with himself in reflection, prayer and meditation. A positive life comes from having hope and faith, and hope and faith come from spending reflective time with yourself.

The first person to spend quality
time with is yourself,
in quiet, with God.
This is the foundation and source
of all else that you want.

Conclusion

Choose one person you know,
one person you don't, and
do something kind for them.
... and don't let them know
it was you.

My hope is that here, at the end of this book, you are finding your heart open, and that you have a deeper understanding for Attitudinal Healing. The best way to ensure that the lessons and experiences of this book continue to grow is to practice the principles in your daily life. If ever you can't think of a reason to smile, know that the solution is with you always: Extend love. If you want to smile from your heart, do something that is incredibly kind, with no emphasis on recognition.

Share kindness, compassion and understanding with those you know and those you don't, and include nature. This is all you need to do to smile.

About the Author

As a psychologist, author and consultant, Dr. Lee Jampolsky is a recognized leader in psychology and human potential. He has served on the medical staff and faculty of respected hospitals and graduate schools, contributed to the personal and spiritual growth of countless individuals around the globe, and consulted with management and CEOs of businesses of all sizes.

Dr. Jampolsky's inspirational books, distance learning, workshops and presentations, and individual programs span the fields of health, business, education, spirituality and psychology. His published books, which have sold hundreds of thousands of copies in more than a dozen languages include: *Smile for No Good Reason, Healing the Addictive Personality, Walking Through Walls, The Art of Trust, Listen to Me: Healing Father Son*

Relationships, Healing Together: Going from Crisis to Calm During Turbulent Times, and *Healing the Addictive Mind.*

Dedicated to helping people discover their own pathways to experiencing the miracle of turning obstacles to opportunities on a daily basis, Dr. Jampolsky's unique approach and easy-to-apply techniques allow people to experience a heartfelt shift in attitude.

Dr. Jampolsky lives in Northern California and has appeared on radio and TV shows spanning the globe. He has been interviewed or quoted by hundreds of publications, including the *Wall Street Journal, Business Week, The Los Angeles Times, Entrepreneur,* and *Women's World.*

What OTHERS are saying...

We purchased a Simple Truths' gift book for our conference in Lisbon, Spain. We also personalized it with a note on the first page about valuing innovation. I've never had such positive feedback on any gift we've given. People just keep talking about how much they valued the book and how perfectly it tied back to our conference message.

— **Michael R. Marcey,** Efficient Capital Management, LLC.

The small inspirational books by Simple Truths are amazing magic! They spark my spirit and energize my soul.

— **Jeff Hughes,** United Airlines

Mr. Anderson, ever since a friend of mine sent me the 212° movie online, I have become a raving fan of Simple Truths. I love and appreciate the positive messages your products convey and I have found many ways to use them. Thank you for your vision.

— **Patrick Shaughnessy,** AVI Communications, Inc.

SMALL BOOKS THAT SPEAK VOLUMES

Be sure to enjoy our complete collection of e-books. You'll discover it's a great way to inspire friends and family, or to thank your best customers and employees.

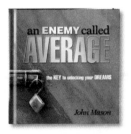

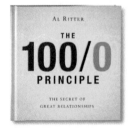

Visit your online book store to find other e-books by Simple Truths

Published by SimpleTruths, LLC
1952 McDowell Road, Suite 300
Naperville, Illinois 60563

Design: Lynn Harker, Simple Truths, Illinois
Edited by: Alice Patenaude, Simple Truths, Illinois

Photo: ThinkStock.com / Shutterstock.com

Simple Truths is a registered trademark.
Printed and bound in the United States of America

ISBN 978-1-60810-188-7

800-900-3427
www.simpletruths.com

01 WOZ 12